Peep This!
Hip Hop Trivia

Volume 1

Peep This!
Hip Hop Trivia

Volume I

By
Joe Youngblood

Published by Smokin' Joe Entertainment
Editorial, sales and distribution, rights and permission inquiries should be addressed to Smokin' Joe Entertainment, 61-23 190th Street, Suite 112, Fresh Meadows, NY 11365

Distributed by
Lightning Source, Inc. and
www.SmokinJoeMedia.com

Peep This! Hip Hop Trivia

ISBN 0-9764047-0-2

Cover design by Bookcovers.com
Page design by Intergrativeink.com

TABLE OF CONTENTS

PREFACE

For years my friends and I would sit and reminisce about hip hop culture. Being an aspiring hip hop producer, I always wanted to know who produced the song and what sample they used. To find out these answers, I would read credits of my album and CD covers. Over the years I realized that I had acquired a lot of knowledge about hip hop. My friends and family would call me whenever they had a question about hip hop artists or songs.

One day a friend of mine was quizzing me on rock n' roll trivia. I was pretty good at it, but not as good as I wanted to be so I purchased a rock n' roll trivia book. While purchasing the rock n' roll trivia book, I decided to pick up a book on hip hop trivia. I found a couple of trivia books on soul/R&B music, which had a few hip hop questions, but I couldn't find one specifically on hip hop. I couldn't believe that a culture with so much history didn't have a trivia book devoted to it. So here it is!

— Joe Youngblood

DEDICATION

This book is dedicated to the memory of my father,
Joseph Youngblood Jr.
1938-2003

ACKNOWLEDGEMENTS

I would like to thank my family and friends for their support on this project. I would like to give a special thanks to my sister JoAnn and my friend Maria for all of their help and encouragement. I would also like to thank Walt Goodridge, the Passion Prophet, for helping me to find another outlet to express my passion for hip hop. In preparing this book, I did extensive research from books, movies, magazines and various websites. *The Vibe History of Hip Hop* edited by Alan Light, *ego trip's Book Of Rap Lists* and *yes yes y'all* by Jim Fricke and Charlie Ahearn are three books that helped me gain more insight into the history of hip hop. Last but not least, I would like to thank everyone that had anything to do with helping to create and prolong this culture because without you this book would not have been possible.

NAMES

Most hip hop artists don't use their real name. They use a rap moniker, which is a nickname. It can be difficult trying to remember everyone's rap moniker and what it stands for. This chapter deals with questions on the names of hip hop artists. See how many of these you can get right.

1. **What is LL Cool J's real name?**

    a. Leroy James Smith

    b. James Thomas Smith

    c. James Todd Smith

2. **What does LL Cool J stand for?**

    a. Ladies Like Cool Joe

    b. Ladies Love Cool James

    c. Ladies Lust Cool Joe

3. **What does EPMD stand for?**

    a. Erick and Parrish Making Dollars

    b. Every Player Makes Dollars

    c. Erick and Parrish Making Deals

4.   What group was Ja Rule in before going solo?

    a.   Da Bush Babies

    b.   Onyx

    c.   Cash Money Click

5.   What rapper's real name is Dante Smith?

    a.   Redman

    b.   Mos Def

    c.   Big Daddy Kane

6.   What does GURU from the group GangStarr stand for?

    a.   Gifted Universal Rhymes Unlimited

    b.   Gifted Unlimited Rhymes Universal

    c.   Gifted Universal Raps Unlimited

7.   What is the name of the rap group that basketball star Shaquille O'Neal make his recording debut with?

    a.   Black Sheep

    b.   Das Efx

    c.   Fu-Schnickens

8. **What is KRS One's real name?**

   a. Lawrence Parker

   b. Kris Parker

   c. Leroy Parker

9. **Before forming Cypress Hill what group was DJ Muggs a member of?**

   a. Digital Underground

   b. Alkaholiks

   c. 7A3

10. **What was the name of Marly Marl's Crew?**

    a. Queensbridge Crew

    b. Juice Crew

    c. Marly's Crew

11. **What was the name of the crew that featured A Tribe Called Quest, De La Soul, and the Jungle Bros.?**

    a. Juice Crew

    b. Native Tongues

    c. Flavor Unit

12. **What group was Producer Easy Mo Bee a member of?**

    a. Rapping is Fundamental (RIF)

    b. Stetsasonic

    c. Brand Nubian

13. **What group's song was Nas featured on before becoming a star?**

    a. A Tribe Called Quest

    b. Main Source

    c. Public Enemy

14. **What is the rapper/actor Ice Cube's real name?**

    a. Isaac Jackson

    b. Kareem Jackson

    c. O'Shea Jackson

15. **What is rapper/actor Queen Latifah's real name?**

    a. Dana Olson

    b. Donna Owens

    c. Dana Owens

16. **Who are the three members of the group Black Moon?**

   a. Buckshot, Mr. Walt, Evil Dee

   b. Buckshot, Phife, Evil Dee

   c. Buckshot, 5ft, Evil Dee

17. **What is Jam Master J's real name?**

   a. Jason Simmons

   b. Joe McDaniels

   c. Jason Mizell

18. **What is Ludacris' real name?**

   a. Chris Jackson

   b. Chris Bridges

   c. Chris Johnson

19. **What is Notorious B.I.G.'s real name?**

   a. Charles Martin

   b. Christopher Walters

   c. Christopher Wallace

20. **What group is Kool Keith a part of?**

   a. Above The Law

   b. Ultramagnetic MC's

   c. Lost Boys

21.   What is Heavy D's real name?

a.   Dwight Myers

b.   Dennis Myers

c.   David Mayer

22.   Who is NOT a member of the Sugarhill Gang?

a.   Scorpio

b.   Wonder Mike

c.   Big Bank Hank

23.   What rap group was Bryce Wilson a member of before R&B group Groove Theory?

a.   Digital Underground

b.   The Pharcyde

c.   Mantronix

24.   What 3 rappers were in a group called Children of the Corn before going in their own directions?

a.   Mase, Cam'ron and Nas

b.   Mase, Nas and Big L

c.   Mase, Cam'ron and Big L

25. **What is Tupac Shakur's middle name?**

    a. Makaveli

    b. Amaru

    c. Akeem

26. **Simone Johnson is better known as ...**

    a. Amerie

    b. Monie Love

    c. MC Lyte

27. **What does UTFO stand for?**

    a. Untouchable Force Organization

    b. Untouchable Freedom Organization

    c. Unstoppable Force Organization

28. **What does BDP stand for?**

    a. Boogie Down Posse

    b. Beat Down Productions

    c. Boogie Down Productions

29. **Crazy Legs, Lenny Len, Mr. Wiggles, Bobbito, Buck 4, Fabel, Lady Jules, Q-Unique, Easy Roc, Tony Touch, Fever 1, Frosty Freeze, Little Crazy Legs, and Ken Swift, are all members and former members of what group?**

   a. Right Steady Crew

   b. Rock Steady Crew

   c. Rock Stop Crew

30. **Who is NOT a member of the Dungeon Family?**

   a. Cool Breeze

   b. Cee Lo

   c. Ludacris

31. **Which of the following is NOT an alias of a member of the Wu-Tang Clan?**

   a. Golden Arms

   b. Osirus

   c. Funk Doc

32. **Which of these is NOT a duo?**

   a. Nice & Smooth

   b. K-Def & Larry O

   c. D-Nice and Smoothe Da Hustler

33. **Which group is NOT a member of the Boot Camp Clik?**

    a. Group Home

    b. Cocoa Brovaz

    c. Heltah Skeltah

34. **Which emcee was NOT a part of The Juice Crew?**

    a. Just Ice

    b. MC Shan

    c. Craig G

35. **Mos Def and Talib Kweli make up what group?**

    a. Audio Two

    b. Def Kweli

    c. Blackstar

36. **Which group was Pharoahe Monch a part of before going solo?**

    a. Onyx

    b. Boogiemonsters

    c. Organized Confusion

37.   **What artist was born Antwon Patton?**

    a. Big Boi

    b. Choclair

    c. Buckshot

38.   **Which of the following are the three Members of the Originoo Gunn Clappaz?**

    a. Ruck, Rock, Mr. Walt

    b. Louieville, Starang, Top Dog

    c. Evil Dee, Starang, Louieville

39.   **What artist was born Cornell Haynes, Jr.?**

    a. Nelly

    b. DJ Yella

    c. Rampage

40.   **What artist was born John Jackson?**

    a. Q-tip

    b. J-Kwon

    c. Fabolous

41.   **What artist was born Terrance Kelly?**

    a. Common

    b. King Tee

    c. Mr. Cheeks

42. **Of the following, which one was a DJ for Stetsasonic?**

    a. Delite

    b. Prince Paul

    c. Fruitkwan

43. **What artist was born Marshall Mathers?**

    a. Everlast

    b. Eminem

    c. Vanilla Ice

44. **What artist was born Malik Cox?**

    a. Scarface

    b. Memphis Bleek

    c. Treach

45. **Who was the original DJ for Boogie Down Productions?**

    a. DJ Polo

    b. Scott LaRock

    c. DJ K La Boss

46. **What artist was born Shawntae Harris?**

    a. Shawna

    b. Da Brat

    c. Ciara

47. **What is Jay-Z's middle name?**

    a. David

    b. Edward

    c. Corey

48. **What artist was born Maurice Young?**

    a. Trick Daddy

    b. Busta Rhymes

    c. Young MC

49. **Which one of these rappers was in the group A Tribe Called Quest?**

    a. Posdnous

    b. Chi Ali

    c. Phife

50. **Which one of these groups do NOT have a set of twins in it?**

   a. Jagged Edge

   b. H-Town

   c. Jodeci

51. **Who is NOT a part of the Ruff Ryders Camp?**

   a. Jadakiss

   b. Jay-Z

   c. DMX

52. **What is the name of Eminem's daughter?**

   a. Mary

   b. Susie

   c. Hailie

53. **What is DMX's real name?**

   a. David Mitchell

   b. Earl Simmons

   c. Don McDaniel

54. **Which group had to change their name to Cocoa Brovaz?**

    a. Nice and Smooth

    b. Smif & Wessun

    c. K-Def & Larry D

55. **What is Jay-Z's real name?**

    a. Shawn Carter

    b. Sean John

    c. Joseph Robinson

56. **What is DJ Quik's real name?**

    a. David Blake

    b. Quinton Wiggins

    c. Deshawn Smith

57. **Nate Dogg, Snoop and Warren G formed which rap group back in the day?**

    a. Compton's Most Wanted

    b. 213

    c. Down By Law

58. **What is another nickname for Redman?**

    a. Funk Doctor Spock

    b. The Funky Child

    c. Mr. Funky Man

59. **Lil' Fame and Billy Danz are ...**

    a. Compton's Most Wanted

    b. Blackstar

    c. M.O.P.

60. **What is N.O.R.E.'s real name?**

    a. Melvin Flynt

    b. Victor Santiago

    c. Paul Anderson

61. **What is Redman's real name?**

    a. Reggie Noble

    b. Maliek Turner

    c. Eric Spencer

62. **Who is NOT a part of the Terror Squad?**

    a. Psycho Les

    b. Prospect

    c. Armageddon

63.   **What was the name of Kool Herc's crew?**

   a.   Crash Crew

   b.   Fantastic Five

   c.   The Herculoids

64.   **Who was the original "Chief Rocker"?**

   a.   Luv Bug Starski

   b.   Busy Bee

   c.   Cowboy

65.   **How was Run originally billed?**

   a.   Jam Master Jay

   b.   DJ Joey

   c.   DJ Run

66.   **What does the "L" stand for in the L Brothers?**

   a.   Lawrence

   b.   Livingston

   c.   Lorenzo

67.   **Which member of Whodini has a twin brother?**

   a.   Jalil

   b.   Ecstasy

   c.   Grandmaster Dee

68. **What rapper was known as "The Love Rapper"?**

    a. Luv Bug Starski

    b. Jimmy Spicer

    c. Spoonie Gee

69. **Who coined the phrase "Yes Yes Ya'll"?**

    a. Luv Bug Starski

    b. Cowboy

    c. Melle Mel

70. **What friend did Kool Herc pull on stage with him to work the crowd and essentially become the first MC?**

    a. Coke La Rock

    b. Busy Bee

    c. Clark Kent

71. **Who is NOT a Zulu Nation DJ.**

    a. Jazzy Jay

    b. Grand Mixer D.ST

    c. AJ Scratch

72. **Which members of the Furious Five are brothers?**

    a. Cowboy and Melle Mel

    b. Melle Mel and Kid Creole

    c. Kid Creole and Scorpio

73. **E-Swift, Tash & J-Ro are who?**

    a. The Boogiemonsters

    b. Above The Law

    c. The Alkaholiks

74. **Who is NOT in the DITC?**

    a. Kid Capri

    b. Fat Joe

    c. Showbiz

75. **What is Kool Herc's real name?**

    a. David Bailey

    b. James King

    c. Clive Campbell

76. **What is Grandmaster Flash's real name?**

    a. William Sarden

    b. Melvin Little

    c. Joseph Saddler

77. **What is Kurtis Blow's real name?**

    a.   Kurt Johnson

    b.   Kurt Daniels

    c.   Kurt Walker

78. **Who is NOT a part of the rap group Sequence?**

    a.   Angie B

    b.   Sha Rock

    c.   Blondie

79. **Who was the DJ for Big Daddy Kane?**

    a.   Mister Cee

    b.   Marly Marl

    c.   Biz Markie

80. **What do Heltah Skeltah and OGC call themselves?**

    a.   Boot Camp's Finest

    b.   Jurassic 5

    c.   Fab Five

81. **Who was the DJ for King Tee?**

    a.   DJ Aladdin

    b.   DJ Pooh

    c.   Cutmaster Cool Vee

82. **Who was the DJ for Leaders of the New School?**

    a. DJ Dinco D

    b. Cut Monitor Milo

    c. DJ Charlie Brown

83. **Who was the DJ for 3rd Bass?**

    a. Prime Minister Pete Nice

    b. Sam Sever

    c. Richie Rich

84. **What is 50 cent's real name?**

    a. John Jackson

    b. Curtis Jackson

    c. Dennis Jackson

85. **What is The Game's real name?**

    a. Joseph Turner

    b. Jayceon Taylor

    c. Terrell Jackson

86. **What Wu-Tang member is a.k.a. Rollie Fingers?**

    a. U-God

    b. Raekwon

    c. Inspectah Deck

87. **What is the real name of Ol' Dirty Bastard?**

    a. Russell Jones

    b. Russell James

    c. Rudolph Jones

88. **What does the G in G-Unit stand for?**

    a. Gangsta

    b. Gotti

    c. Guerilla

89. **Which of these rappers real name is Trevor Smith?**

    a. Method Man

    b. Busta Rhymes

    c. Ras Kass

90. Which of these rappers real name is William Griffin?

    a. Slim Thug

    b. Rakim

    c. Kool G Rap

91. What does the name of the group M.O.P. stand for?

    a. Marcy's Own Productions

    b. Mobbed Out Posse

    c. Mash Out Posse

92. What 2 rappers make up the group The Beatnuts?

    a. Psycho Les and JoJo

    b. Psycho Lev and JoJo

    c. Psycho Les and JuJu

93. What is Jeffrey Townes rap moniker?

    a. Ja Rule

    b. Jazzy Jeff

    c. Def Jef

94. **What is the real name of the rapper Jadakiss?**

    a. Jason Phillips

    b. James Wallace

    c. John Wallace

95. **What is the real name of the rapper T.I.?**

    a. Clifford Harris

    b. Clifford Smith

    c. Christopher Jenkins

96. **Which one of these is NOT a nickname of Ol' Dirty Bastard**

    a. Osirus

    b. The Abbott

    c. Big Baby Jesus

97. **Terius Gray is the real name of which rapper?**

    a. Spice 1

    b. MC Eight

    c. Juvenile

98. **What rapper's real name is Shad Moss?**

    a. Ghostface

    b. Bow Wow

    c. Lil' Scrappy

99. **What rapper's real name is Carl Mitchell?**

    a.   Twista

    b.   Common

    c.   Cassidy

100. **What is the real name of MC Lyte?**

    a.   Stacy Thompson

    b.   Lana Moorer

    c.   Latoya Jones

101. **What rapper's real name is Kenyatta Blake?**

    a.   Buckshot

    b.   Prodigy

    c.   Guerilla Black

ANSWERS FOR NAMES

1. c. James Todd Smith
2. b. Ladies Love Cool James
3. a. Erick and Parrish Making Dollars
4. c. Cash Money Click
5. b. Mos Def
6. b. Gifted Unlimited Rhymes Universal
7. c. Fu-Schnickens
8. a. Lawrence Parker
9. c. 7A3
10. b. Juice Crew
11. b. Native Tongues
12. a. Rapping is Fundamental (RIF)
13. b. Main Source
14. c. O'Shea Jackson
15. c. Dana Owens
16. c. Buckshot, 5ft, Evil Dee
17. c. Jason Mizell
18. b. Chris Bridges
19. c. Christopher Wallace
20. b. Ultramagnetic MC's
21. a. Dwight Myers
22. a. Scorpio
23. c. Mantronix
24. c. Mase, Cam'ron, and Big L
25. b. Amaru
26. b. Monie Love
27. a. Untouchable Force Organization
28. c. Boogie Down Productions
29. b. Rock Steady Crew
30. c. Ludacris
31. c. Funk Doc
32. c. D-Nice and Smoothe Da Hustler
33. a. Group Home
34. a. Just Ice

35.   c. Blackstar
36.   c. Organized Confusion
37.   a. Big Boi
38.   b. Louieville, Starang, Top Dog
39.   a. Nelly
40.   c. Fabolous
41.   c. Mr. Cheeks
42.   b. Prince Paul
43.   b. Eminem
44.   b. Memphis Bleek
45.   b. Scott LaRock
46.   b. Da Brat
47.   c. Corey
48.   a. Trick Daddy
49.   c. Phife
50.   c. Jodeci
51.   b. Jay-Z
52.   c. Hailie
53.   b. Earl Simmons
54.   b. Smif & Wessun
55.   a. Shawn Carter
56.   a. David Blake
57.   b. 213
58.   a. Funk Doctor Spock
59.   c. M.O.P.
60.   b. Victor Santiago
61.   a. Reggie Noble
62.   a. Psycho Les
63.   c. The Herculoids
64.   b. Busy Bee
65.   c. DJ Run, son of Kurtis Blow
66.   b. Livingston
67.   b. Ecstasy
68.   a. Luv Bug Starski
69.   b. Cowboy
70.   a. Coke La Rock
71.   c. AJ Scratch

72.	b. Melle Mel and Kid Creole [Glover]
73.	c. The Alkaholiks
74.	a. Kid Capri
75.	c. Clive Campbell
76.	c. Joseph Saddler
77.	c. Kurt Walker
78.	b. Sha Rock
79.	a. Mister Cee
80.	c. Fab Five
81.	b. DJ Pooh
82.	b. Cut Monitor Milo
83.	c. Richie Rich
84.	b. Curtis Jackson
85.	b. Jayceon Taylor
86.	c. Inspectah Deck
87.	a. Russell Jones
88.	c. Guerilla
89.	b. Busta Rhymes
90.	b. Rakim
91.	c. Mash Out Posse
92.	c. Psycho Les and JuJu
93.	b. Jazzy Jeff
94.	a. Jason Phillips
95.	a. Clifford Harris
96.	b. The Abbott
97.	c. Juvenile
98.	b. Bow Wow
99.	a. Twista
100.	b. Lana Moorer
101.	a. Buckshot

BEATS

Hip hop music takes different styles of music and blends it together. In most cases, it is created by using a technology called sampling. Sampling is the process of taking a musical phrase from one recording and using it in another. What album did a certain single come from and what sample it used are some of the questions you will find in this chapter. See how much you know about the hip hop songs you love.

102. **What year did LL Cool J come out with his first single?**

    a. 1985

    b. 1984

    c. 1986

103. **What group's song was featured as the theme song for *Video Music Box*?**

    a. Whodini

    b. UTFO

    c. Run DMC

104. **What song did LL Cool J perform in *Krush Groove*?**

a. "Radio"

b. "I Need a Beat"

c. "Rock the Bells"

105. **Who produced "Roxanne's Revenge"?**

a. Red Alert

b. Teddy Riley

c. Marly Marl

106. **What is the name of the song LL Cool J did with EPMD?**

a. "Crossover"

b. "Headbanger"

c. "Rampage"

107. **What rapper did NOT perform on "The Symphony"?**

a. Biz Markie

b. Masta Ace

c. Big Daddy Kane

108. **Who said "F**k Compton"?**

    a. Ice Cube

    b. Tim Dog

    c. KRS-One

109. **Who stated "Who Da Cap Fits"?**

    a. Shabba Ranks

    b. Just-Ice

    c. Shinehead

110. **What is the name of De La Soul's first single?**

    a. "Plug Tunin' "

    b. "Me, Myself & I"

    c. "Potholes In My Lawn"

111. **What is Notorious B.I.G.'s first song?**

    a. "Juicy"

    b. "One More Chance"

    c. "Party and Bullsh*t"

112. **Who stated "Be A Father To Your Child"?**

    a. Nas

    b. Ed OG and Da Bulldogs

    c. Grand Daddy IU

113. **What song did Queen Latifah record that empowers women?**

   a. "Girl Power"

   b. "Sister, Sister"

   c. "Ladies First"

114. **Who wrote the song "Rapture" by Blondie?**

   a. Debbie Harry

   b. Jean Michel Basquiat

   c. Fab Five Freddy

115. **Who had a single called "The Jump Off"?**

   a. Missy

   b. Lil' Kim

   c. Eve

116. **Who appears on Missy Elliot's "Gossip Folks"?**

   a. Timbaland

   b. Ludacris

   c. Nas

117. **Which rapper boasts "I Can"?**

    a. DMX

    b. Jay Z

    c. Nas

118. **"Sing For The Moment" is a hit of which rapper?**

    a. Jay-Z

    b. Eminem

    c. Nelly

119. **Who had hits with "Awnaw" and "Po' Folks"?**

    a. Killer Mike

    b. Nappy Roots

    c. Method Man

120. **Which artist raps "Thug Lovin'" and "Mesmerize"?**

    a. Nas

    b. Ja Rule

    c. Tupac

121. **Jay-Z and Mary J. Blige did what song together on *Reasonable Doubt*?**

    a. "Can't Knock the Hustle"

    b. "Ain't No Nigga"

    c. "Feelin It"

122. **Notorious B.I.G. and 112, did what song together on B.I.G.'s *Life After Death* album?**

    a. "Notorious Thugs'

    b. "Player Hater"

    c. "Sky's the Limit"

123. **Nas and Lauryn Hill did what song together on Nas' *It Was Written*?**

    a. "Street Dreams"

    b. "If I Ruled the World"

    c. "Black Girl Lost"

124. **Nelly and Kelly Rowland did what song together on *Nellyville*?**

    a. "Oh Nelly"

    b. "Work It"

    c. "Dilemma"

125. **Wyclef and Mary J. Blige did what song together on Wyclef's *The Ecleftic*?**

    a. "Two Wrongs"

    b. "Knockin' on Heaven's Door"

    c. "911"

126. **Ghostface and Carl Thomas did what song together on *Bulletproof Wallets*?**

    a. "Ghost Showers"

    b. "Never Be the Same Again"

    c. "Love Session"

127. **R. Kelly and Keith Murray did what song together on *R.*?**

    a. "Did You Ever Think"

    b. "Spendin' Money"

    c. "Home Alone"

128. **Mary J. Blige and Ja Rule did what song together on *No More Drama*?**

    a. "Steal Away"

    b. "Rainy Dayz"

    c. "Family Affair"

129. **Mya and Jadakiss did what song together on Mya's *Fear of Flying*?**

   a. "Case of the Ex"

   b. "Best of Me"

   c. "Man of My Life"

130. **Beyoncé and Jay-Z did what song together on *Dangerously In Love*?**

   a. "Baby Boy"

   b. "Naughty Girl"

   c. "Crazy In Love"

131. **Faith Evans and P. Diddy did what song together on *Keep The Faith*?**

   a. "You Used To Love Me"

   b. "Love Like This"

   c. "All Night Long"

132. **J. Lo and Ja Rule did what song together on *Irv Gotti Presents ...*?**

   a. "I'm Real"

   b. "All I Have"

   c. "Ain't It Funny"

133. **R. Kelly and Big Tigger did what song together on Kelly's *Chocolate Factory*?**

    a. "Snake"

    b. "When a Woman's Fed Up"

    c. "If I Could Turn Back the Hands of Time"

134. **Dr. Dre and Mary J. Blige did what song together on *Chronic 2001*?**

    a. "Message"

    b. "Xxpolsive"

    c. "The Next Episode"

135. **Which producer sings the chorus on Nas' "The World Is Yours"?**

    a. Pete Rock

    b. Large Professor

    c. Q-Tip

136. **Which of these songs was NOT produced by DJ Premier?**

    a. "The 6th Sense"

    b. "Wild for the Night"

    c. "NY State of Mind"

137. **For one of her hits, what female artist sampled the song "Chic Cheer"?**

   a. Mary J. Blige

   b. Ashanti

   c. Faith Evans

138. **What is the name of the song sampled by Vanilla Ice in his hit "Ice, Ice, Baby"**

   a. "Under Pressure"

   b. "Cold As Ice"

   c. "Jive Talkin'"

139. **Foxy Brown and Jay-Z recorded a song entitled "I'll Be Good" Which eighties group originally recorded the song?**

   a. Rene and Angela

   b. SOS Band

   c. Midnight Star

140. **A remix of "Get Money" by Junior Mafia and Notorious B.I.G sampled the song "Don't Look Any Further" by which artists?**

   a. Dennis Edwards and Shirley Murdock

   b. Dennis Edwards and Stephanie Mills

   c. Dennis Edwards and Siedah Garrett

141. Rapper Ahmad had a hit with the song "Back in the Day." From which Teddy Pendergrass song did he get the beat?

    a. "Turn Off the Lights"

    b. "Close the Door"

    c. "Love T.K.O."

142. For his song "What Means the World to You" rapper Cam'ron sampled which pop group?

    a. Duran Duran

    b. U2

    c. The Police

143. Run DMC sampled Aerosmith for their smash hit "Walk This Way." What year did the original Aerosmith recording come out?

    a. 1974

    b. 1975

    c. 1976

144. What was the first single from Smif´n´Wessuns' debut LP *Dah Shinin*?

    a. "Lets Get It On"

    b. "Bucktown"

    c. "Sound Boy Burial"

145. Jay-Z's "Sunshine" which featured vocals by Babyface and Foxy Brown used a sample from what eighties rap group?

    a. Crash Crew

    b. Funky 4 + 1

    c. Fearless Four

146. What is the title of the Debarge song Biggie used for his hit "One More Chance"?

    a. "All This Love"

    b. "Stay With Me"

    c. "Wear It Well"

147. J. Lo made a song with LL Cool J in which she sang all my love is "All I Have" Who originally sung this in their song?

    a. Peaches & Herb

    b. Ronnie & Debra Laws

    c. Yarborough & Peoples

148. Which Mariah Carey song sampled the beat from "Genius Of Love"?

    a. "Heartbreaker"

    b. "Honey"

    c. "Fantasy"

149. From what group did Will Smith sample the beat for his song "Gettin' Jiggy With It"?

    a. Cameo

    b. Sister Sledge

    c. Dazz Band

150. For her song "I Can't" featuring Total, Foxy Brown used a sample from which group?

    a. Wham

    b. Duran Duran

    c. Culture Club

151. On *The Chronic* album, Dr. Dre sampled Parliament on the song "Let Me Ride." Which song did the sample come from?

    a. "Flashlight"

    b. "Mothership Connection (Star Child)"

    c. "Atomic Dog"

152. What was the name of the song sampled in the Bad Boy Hit "Mo Money, Mo Problems" by Biggie, Puffy and Mase?

    a. "I'm Coming Out"

    b. "Give It To Me Baby"

    c. "We are Family"

153. The song "It Was A Good Day" by Ice Cube sampled which song?

    a. "Between the Sheets"

    b. "Footsteps in the Dark"

    c. "At Your Best"

154. What is Run-DMC's 5th album titled?

    a. "Down with the King"

    b. "Crown Royal"

    c. "Back From Hell"

155. Who is kickin' brand new "Flava In Your Ear"?

    a. Craig Mack

    b. Flava Flav

    c. Busta Rhymes

156. What year was N.W.A.'s *Straight Outta Compton* album released?

    a. 1986

    b. 1887

    c. 1988

157. **Which group made the song "Music Makes Me High"?**

    a. Onyx

    b. Cypress Hill

    c. Lost Boys

158. **Who produced The Notorious B.I.G.'s song "Unbelievable"?**

    a. Easy Mo Bee

    b. Pete Rock

    c. DJ Premier

159. **Who sung "Humpty Dance"?**

    a. Digital Underground

    b. Pharcyde

    c. Mc Hammer

160. **Who sung "6 'N The Mornin'"?**

    a. Easy E

    b. Ice-T

    c. Schooly D

161. **Who sung "Saturday Night"?**

    a. Schooly D

    b. Ice Cube

    c. Geto Boys

162. **Who sung "Glamorous Life"?**

    a. Stezo

    b. Cool C.

    c. Steady B

163. **Who sung "Party For Your Right To Fight"?**

    a. Beastie Boys

    b. Public Enemy

    c. The Boogie Monsters

164. **Who sung "Joy And Pain"?**

    a. Rob Base & DJ EZ Rock

    b. Pete Rock & CL Smooth

    c. Stetsasonic

165. **Who sung "Proud To Be Black"?**

    a. Public Enemy

    b. X-Clan

    c. Run DMC

166. **Who sung "Raw"?**

    a. Just Ice

    b. Big Daddy Kane

    c. Doug E Fresh

167. **Who sung "Rock The Bells"?**

    a. LL Cool J

    b. Jazzy Jeff & The Fresh Prince

    c. Jungle Brothers

168. **Who sung "Jack of Spades"?**

    a. Kool Mo Dee

    b. BDP

    c. Paris

169. **Who sung "Mona Lisa"?**

    a. Slick Rick

    b. Dana Dane

    c. Kurtis Blow

170. **Who sung "Gas Face"?**

    a. Beastie Boys

    b. Jazzy Jeff & The Fresh Prince

    c. 3rd Bass

171. **Who said "I Left My Wallet In El Segundo"?**

    a. Cypress Hill

    b. A Tribe Called Quest

    c. De La Soul

172. **Which two artists made a good duet back in the old days with "Your All I Need"?**

    a. Method Man & Mary J. Blige

    b. Q-tip & Janet Jackson

    c. Jay-Z & Foxy Brown

173. **Who does Dr. Dre work with on "Forgot About Dre"?**

    a. Snoop Dogg

    b. Nate Dogg

    c. Eminem

174. **What rapper is featured on "Big Ego's" by Dr. Dre?**

    a. Warren G

    b. Hitman

    c. Kurupt

175. **What was the name of Domino's 1993 hit?**

    a. "Ghetto Jam"

    b. "Keep It"

    c. "Let's Get High"

176. **What is the state that Arrested Development rapped about in 1992?**

    a. "Tennessee"

    b. "Atlanta"

    c. "Arizona"

177. **Name the LL Cool J song that shares the same name as an Easy E song.**

    a. "Rock the Bells"

    b. "Radio"

    c. "To Da Break Of Dawn"

178. **Which of the following is on Nelly's *Country Grammar* CD?**

    a. "Hot In Herre"

    b. "E.I."

    c. "# 1"

179. **Which of these is NOT a Juvenile CD?**

    a. *G-Code*

    b. *The Block is Hot*

    c. *Project English*

180. Who did the song "Just A Friendly Game Of Baseball"?

    a. Naughty By Nature

    b. Black Sheep

    c. Main Source

181. This group had a few singles such as "Chief Rocka", "Funky Child", and "Here come the Lords"?

    a. The Lords of Rap

    b. Lords of the Underground

    c. Ghetto Lords

182. What song does Jeru the Damaja and Lil Dap appear on GangStarr's *Daily Operation* CD?

    a. "Soliloquy of Chaos"

    b. "Speak Ya Clout"

    c. "I'm the Man"

183. Eazy E released *Eazy-Duz-It* in what year?

    a. 1986

    b. 1987

    c. 1988

184. **Which artist is NOT on "Self Destruction"?**

    a. Kool Moe Dee

    b. Slick Rick

    c. Heavy D

185. **The West Coast did a song called "We All In The Same Gang." Which artist appeared on that?**

    a. 2pac

    b. MC Ren

    c. Ice Cube

186. **Public Enemy did what song for the movie *Do The Right Thing?***

    a. "Fight the Power"

    b. "Welcome To The Terrordome"

    c. "Don't Believe The Hype"

187. **What song on Jay-Z's album *Reasonable Doubt* featured The Notorious B.I.G.?**

    a. "Brooklyn's In Da House"

    b. "Brooklyn's Finest"

    c. "D' Evils"

188. **Who was the only MC featured on Eazy E's album *Eazy-Duz-It?***

    a. Ice Cube

    b. MC Ren

    c. Dr. Dre

189. **What was DJ Quik's 1991 debut album titled?**

    a. *Born & Raised In Compton*

    b. *My Name Is Quik*

    c. *Quik Is The Name*

190. **Who did Naughty By Nature NOT give a shout out to in "Hip Hop Hooray"?**

    a. Nice and Smooth

    b. De La Soul

    c. Leaders of the New School

191. **Which EPMD song was Redman first featured?**

    a. "Rampage"

    b. "Crossover"

    c. "Hardcore"

192. **Who told us to "Go See The Doctor" back in 1987?**

    a. Slick Rick

    b. Kool Moe Dee

    c. Just Ice

193. **What rap group performed the "Wrestlemania Rap"?**

    a. EPMD

    b. Run DMC

    c. Jazzy Jeff & The Fresh Prince

194. **Which of these rap artists is NOT featured on the "I Shot Ya" remix by LL Cool J?**

    a. Prodigy

    b. Foxy Brown

    c. Canibus

195. **Mobb Deep's first album is called...**

    a. *Juvenile Delinquents*

    b. *Juvenile Hell*

    c. *Delinquents From Hell*

196. **Who was the guest artist on Redman's "Watch Yo' Nugget"?**

a. K-Solo

b. PMD

c. Erick Sermon

197. **Who released the album The Sun Rises In The East?**

a. Jeru the Damaja

b. Wu Tang Clan

c. King Sun

198. **Who was the guest artist on Nas' song "Life's a Bitch"?**

a. AZ

b. Q-Tip

c. Notorious B.I.G.

199. **Name the tune that had a John Wayne impersonator rapping the entire song.**

a. "Do The John Wayne"

b. "Rappin' John"

c. "Rappin' Duke"

200. This rapper/actor's songs include "(So U Wanna Be) Hardcore", "Way It's Goin' Down (T.W.IsM. for Life)", "I'm Outstanding". Name him.

   a. Ice-T

   b. Ice Cube

   c. Shaquille O'Neal

201. This group debuted with the album called *21 and Over*?

   a. Wrecks & Effect

   b. The Clipse

   c. The Alkaholiks

202. This group featured KRS-One on the single "Mad Izm"?

   a. Channel Live

   b. Cypress Hill

   c. Da Bush Babees

203. This group had the single "Hand On The Pump"?

   a. The Alkaholiks

   b. Cypress Hill

   c. 3rd Bass

204. **For what movie soundtrack did Dr. Dre first introduce Snoop Doggy Dogg?**

a. *Trespass*

b. *Boyz N' The Hood*

c. *Deep Cover*

205. **Which one of these songs was sung by Pharoahe Monch?**

a. "You Played Yourself"

b. "Simon Says"

c. "Just to Get a Rep"

206. **Who sings "Ha"?**

a. Master P

b. Juvenile

c. Trick Daddy

207. **Which one of the following songs do Shade Sheist, Kurupt and Nate Dogg rap together on?**

a. "Up In The Hood"

b. "Where I Wanna Be"

c. "Ganstas & Playas"

208. **Who is featured in Mobb Deep's song "Quiet Storm"?**

    a.   Lil' Kim

    b.   Eve

    c.   Foxy Brown

209. **What was Kurtis Blow's first record?**

    a.   "Christmas Rappin'"

    b.   "The Breaks"

    c.   "Superrappin"

210. **What James Brown record is considered by many to be the B-boy anthem?**

    a.   "Give it Up or Turn it Loose"

    b.   "Funky Drummer"

    c.   "Funky President"

211. **Who wrote lyrics for "Rapper's Delight" but never received credit?**

    a.   Melle Mel

    b.   Kool Moe Dee

    c.   Grandmaster Caz

212. **The Whodini song "Magic's Wand" was a tribute to whom?**

   a. Mr. Magic

   b. Magic Johnson

   c. David Copperfield

213. **What record was the source of the "Oh My God!" on Doug E. Fresh's classic "The Show"?**

   a. Master Don Committee's "Funk Box Party"

   b. Cold Crush Brother's "Punk Rock Rap"

   c. Sequence's " Funk You Up"

214. **Who does NOT perform on the song "Krush Groovin" in film *Krush Groove*?**

   a. Fat Boys

   b. Run DMC

   c. Dr. Jekyll & Mr. Hyde

215. **Who remixed Jeru tha Damaja's "Can't Stop the Prophet" in 1994?**

   a. Pete Rock

   b. Large Professor

   c. Easy Mo Bee

216. **Which of the following posse cuts has Big Punisher NOT appeared on?**

    a. "Off Tha Books"

    b. "Tri Boro Trilogy"

    c. "I Shot Ya remix"

217. **Which 4 emcees blessed the mic on the Main Source classic "Live At The Barbecue"?**

    a. Large Professor, Nas, Az, and Joe the Butcher

    b. Large Professor, Nas, Q-Tip and Akinyele

    c. Large Professor, Akinyele, Nas and Joe Fatal

218. **Which track sampled Steely Dan's "Black Cow"?**

    a. "Déjà Vu" by Lord Tariq & Peter Gunz

    b. "Uptown Anthem" by Naughty by Nature

    c. "The Choice Is Yours" by Black Sheep

219. **Who produced O.C.'s 1994 classic "Times Up"?**

    a. Buckwild

    b. Showbiz

    c. DJ Premier

220. Which single was Run DMC's first to be released?

a. "Walk This Way"

b. "It's Like That"

c. "King of Rock"

221. What was LL Cool J's first album?

a. *Mama Said Knock You Out*

b. *Radio*

c. *Bigger and Deffer*

222. What Michael Jackson song does Fabolous use on his song "Baby"?

a. "Human Nature"

b. "I Just Can't Stop Loving You"

c. "I Can't Help It."

223. Twista had a hit with the song "Overnight Celebrity" which was produced by Kanye West. Whose song was sampled?

a. Lenny Williams

b. Al Green

c. Major Harris

224. **Which group did PM Dawn sample for their hit "Set Adrift On Memory Bliss"?**

   a. The Police

   b. Spandau Ballet

   c. The Pet Shop Boys

225. **P. Diddy's "I'll Be Missing You", was dedicated to the late Notorious B.I.G. What was the name of the song this beat came from?**

   a. "Every Step You Take"

   b. "Every Breath You Take"

   c. "I'll Be Watching You"

226. **Kanye West's song "All Falls Down" samples a song from Lauryn Hill. What song is sampled?**

   a. "Doo Wop (That Thing)"

   b. "Just Like Water"

   c. "Mystery of Iniquity"

227. **The song "Threat" on *The Black Album* by Jay-Z samples a song from R&B artist R. Kelly. What song is sampled?**

   a. "When a Woman's Fed Up"

   b. "A Woman's Threat"

   c. "Down Low"

228. **Mr. Cheeks' song "Lights, Camera, Action" was a big hit. Which song was used to get the beat?**

    a. "Keep On Truckin'"

    b. "Boogie Down"

    c. "Boogie Nights"

229. **Dr. Dre and Snoop Doggy Dogg's "Nuthin' But A G Thang" song borrowed the beat from which artist?**

    a. Leon Haywood

    b. Johnnie "J.T." Taylor

    c. Bobby Womack

230. **From which song did Coolio get the beat for his song "Gangsta's Paradise"?**

    a. "Pastime Paradise"

    b. "Part-time Paradise"

    c. "Love's Paradise"

231. **For the song "Hypnotize", the Notorious B.I.G sampled which artist?**

    a. Al Jarreau

    b. Najee

    c. Herb Alpert

232. **From which diva did Kanye West get the sample for his song "Through The Wire"?**

    a. Deniece Williams

    b. Chaka Khan

    c. Anita Baker

233. **From which rap artist did J. Lo get the beat for her song "Ain't It Funny"?**

    a. Craig Mack

    b. Notorious B.I.G

    c. Busta Rhymes

234. **From which group did Notorious B.I.G get the beat for his song "Juicy"?**

    a. Pointer Sisters

    b. Gap Band

    c. Mtume

235. **Before he was known as Diddy, Puffy and Mase made a song entitled "Feel So Good." It included a sample of which song?**

    a. "Jungle Boogie"

    b. "Hollywood Swingin'"

    c. "Word Up"

236. **"Going Back To Cali" and "Bring The Noise" is from which of these movie soundtracks?**

    a. *Pump Up The Volume*

    b. *Less Than Zero*

    c. *Colors*

237. **"Tonight" and "Born and Raised In Compton" is from which of these albums?**

    a. *Straight Outta Compton*

    b. *Quik Is The Name*

    c. *Eazy-Duz-It*

238. **"Bring The Pain" and "Release Yo Delf" is from which of these albums?**

    a. *Enter The 36 Chambers*

    b. *Only Built For Cuban Linx*

    c. *Tical*

239. **"It's Mine", "Streets Raised Me" and "Where Ya Heart At?" is from which album?**

    a. *Stillmatic*

    b. *Nastradamus*

    c. *Murda Muzik*

240. **What song did Biz Markie make his recording debut on?**

    a. "Get Retarded"

    b. "Just Rhymin' With Biz"

    c. "Def Fresh Crew"

241. **Who produced LL Cool J's "Mama Said Knock You Out"?**

    a. Rick Rubin

    b. Pete Rock

    c. Marly Marl

242. **Pete Rock & CL Smooth's song "When They Reminisce Over You" is dedicated to?**

    a. 2pac

    b. Martin Luther King

    c. Trouble T-Roy

243. **Who sung "Good Vibrations"**

    a. Vanilla Ice

    b. KC Flight

    c. Marky Mark and the Funky Bunch

244.   Which group recorded "Rapper's Delight"?

    a.   Funky 4 + 1

    b.   Grandmaster Flash

    c.   Sugarhill Gang

245.   Who performs the female rap verse on The Roots' "You Got Me"?

    a.   Eve

    b.   Foxy Brown

    c.   Erykah Badu

246.   Before B.I.G.'s version, "Going Back To Cali" was recorded by which Def Jam legend?

    a.   Chuck D

    b.   LL Cool J

    c.   Redman

247.   Heltah Skeltah's debut LP has which of the following names?

    a.   *Magnum Force*

    b.   *Manson Family*

    c.   *Nocturnal*

248. **Which artist does A Tribe Called Quest NOT feature on "Scenario"?**

a. Busta Rhymes

b. Posdnuos

c. Charlie Brown

249. **Who is the "Smooth Operator"?**

a. Q-Tip

b. MC Shan

c. Big Daddy Kane

250. **This MC dropped an album called *Power*?**

a. Kool Moe Dee

b. Ice-T

c. KRS-One

251. **They call him "Sooperman Luva"?**

a. Big Daddy Kane

b. Cam'ron

c. Redman

252. **Who was the first hip hop artist to collaborate with a jazz artist on wax?**

a. GangStarr

b. Grand Mixer D.ST

c. Kurtis Blow

253. **Who was the first rap group to use Billy Squire's "Big Beat"?**

    a. Run DMC

    b. UTFO

    c. Whodini

254. **Name Common's debut album.**

    a. *Resurrection*

    b. *Chi-Town's Greatest*

    c. *Can I Borrow A Dollar?*

255. **Name Mad Skillz debut album.**

    a. *The Nod Factor*

    b. *Mad Skillz Is the Name*

    c. *From Where???*

256. **In what year did Eightball and MJG's *On The Outside Looking In* CD come out?**

    a. 1994

    b. 1995

    c. 1996

257. **What was the theme song for** *Video Music Box*?

    a. "Funky Beat"

    b. "Five Minutes to Funk"

    c. "Friends"

258. **Who co-wrote "Wild Thing" with Tone Loc?**

    a. Young MC

    b. Ice-T.

    c. Ice Cube

259. **Before his days with Wu-Tang Clan, what member said "Girl Come Do Me"?**

    a. Method Man

    b. The Genius/Gza

    c. Prince Rakeem/Rza

260. **What is the name of De La Soul's first album?**

    a. *Me, Myself and I*

    b. *3 Feet High and Rising*

    c. *De La Soul Is Dead*

261.   **Who performed the song "Pee Wee Herman Dance"?**

a.   Red-Hot Lover Tone

b.   Audio Two

c.   Joe Ski Love

262.   **What group's song was Nas featured on before becoming a star?**

a.   A Tribe Called Quest

b.   Main Source

c.   Public Enemy

263.   **Who said, "I Used To Love H.E.R."?**

a.   Lord Finesse

b.   Smoothe Da Hustler

c.   Common Sense

264.   **What was BDP's first single?**

a.   Poetry

b.   The South Bronx

c.   The Bridge is Over

265. **Who is NOT featured on Biggie's album *Life After Death*?**

    a. Method Man

    b. R. Kelly

    c. Nas

266. **Black Sheep's debut album was called what?**

    a. *The Black Sheep of the Family*

    b. *Counting Sheep*

    c. *A Wolf in Sheep's Clothing*

267. **What label released "Rockin' It"?**

    a. Enjoy Records

    b. Sugar Hill

    c. Winley

268. **What was Rampage the Last Boyscout's first album called?**

    a. *Take It 2 Da Streets*

    b. *The Red Oktoba*

    c. *Return of the Rampsack*

269. **Who produced the hit "Hot In Herre" by Nelly?**

    a. Trackmasters

    b. Organized Noize

    c. The Neptunes

ANSWERS FOR BEATS

102.	b. 1984
103.	a. Whodini
104.	a. "Radio"
105.	c. Marly Marl
106.	c. "Rampage"
107.	a. Biz Markie
108.	b. Tim Dog
109.	c. Shinehead
110.	a. "Plug Tunin'"
111.	c. "Party and Bullsh*t"
112.	b. Ed OG and Da Bulldogs
113.	c. "Ladies First"
114.	b. Jean Michel Basquiat
115.	b. Lil' Kim
116.	b. Ludacris
117.	c. Nas
118.	b. Eminem
119.	b. Nappy Roots
120.	b. Ja Rule
121.	a. "Can't Knock The Hustle"
122.	c. "Sky's The Limit"
123.	b. "If I Ruled The World"
124.	c. "Dilemma"
125.	c. "911"
126.	b. "Never Be the Same Again"
127.	c. "Home Alone"
128.	b. "Rainy Dayz"
129.	b. "Best Of Me"
130.	c. "Crazy In Love"
131.	c. "All Night Long"
132.	c. "Ain't It Funny"
133.	a. "Snake"
134.	a. "Message"
135.	a. Pete Rock

136.	b. "Wild For The Night"
137.	c. Faith Evans
138.	a. "Under Pressure"
139.	a. Rene and Angela
140.	c. Dennis Edwards and Siedah Garrett
141.	c. "Love T.K.O."
142.	c. The Police
143.	b. 1975
144.	b. "Bucktown"
145.	c. Fearless Four
146.	b. "Stay With Me"
147.	b. Ronnie & Debra Laws
148.	c. "Fantasy"
149.	b. Sister Sledge
150.	a. Wham
151.	b. "Mothership Connection (Star Child)"
152.	a. "I'm Coming Out"
153.	b. "Footsteps in the Dark"
154.	c. *Back From Hell*
155.	a. Craig Mack
156.	c. 1988
157.	c. Lost Boys
158.	c. DJ Premier
159.	a. Digital Underground
160.	b. Ice-T
161.	a. Schooly D
162.	b. Cool C.
163.	b. Public Enemy
164.	a. Rob Base & DJ E-Z Rock
165.	c. Run DMC
166.	b. Big Daddy Kane
167.	a. LL Cool J
168.	b. BDP
169.	a. Slick Rick
170.	c. 3rd Bass
171.	b. A Tribe Called Quest
172.	a. Method Man & Mary J. Blige

173. c. Eminem
174. b. Hitman
175. a. "Ghetto Jam"
176. a. "Tennessee"
177. b. "Radio"
178. b. "E.I."
179. b. *The Block Is Hot*
180. c. Main Source
181. b. Lords of the Underground
182. c. "I'm the Man"
183. c. 1988
184. b. Slick Rick
185. b. MC Ren
186. a. "Fight the Power"
187. b. "Brooklyn's Finest"
188. b. MC Ren
189. c. *Quik Is The Name*
190. b. De La Soul
191. c. "Hardcore"
192. b. Kool Moe Dee
193. b. Run DMC
194. c. Canibus
195. b. *Juvenile Hell*
196. c. Erick Sermon
197. a. Jeru the Damaja
198. a. AZ
199. c. "Rappin Duke"
200. c. Shaquille O'Neal
201. c. The Alkaholiks
202. a. Channel Live
203. b. Cypress Hill
204. c. *Deep Cover*
205. b. "Simon Says"
206. b. Juvenile
207. b. "Where I Wanna Be"
208. a. Lil' Kim
209. a. "Christmas Rappin'"

210.   a. "Give it Up or Turn it Loose"
211.   c. Grandmaster Caz
212.   a. Mr. Magic
213.   b. Cold Crush Brother's "Punk Rock Rap"
214.   c. Dr. Jekyll & Mr. Hyde
215.   a. Pete Rock
216.   c. "I Shot Ya remix"
217.   c. Large Professor, Akinyele, Nas and Joe Fatal
218.   a. "Déjà Vu" by Lord Tariq & Peter Gunz
219.   a. Buckwild
220.   b. "It's Like That"
221.   b. *Radio*
222.   c. "I Can't Help It."
223.   a. Lenny Williams
224.   b. Spandau Ballet
225.   b. "Every Breath You Take"
226.   c. "Mystery of Iniquity"
227.   b. "A Woman's Threat"
228.   a. "Keep On Truckin'"
229.   b. Leon Haywood
230.   a. "Pastime Paradise"
231.   c. Herb Alpert
232.   b. Chaka Khan
233.   a. Craig Mack
234.   c. Mtume
235.   b. "Hollywood Swingin'"
236.   b. *Less Than Zero*
237.   b. *Quik Is The Name*
238.   c. *Tical*
239.   c. *Murda Muzik*
240.   c. "Def Fresh Crew"
241.   c. Marly Marl
242.   c. Trouble T-Roy
243.   c. Marky Mark and the Funky Bunch
244.   c. Sugarhill Gang
245.   a. Eve
246.   b. LL Cool J

247.	c. *Nocturnal*
248.	b. Posdnuos
249.	c. Big Daddy Kane
250.	b. Ice-T
251.	c. Redman
252.	b. Grand Mixer D.ST
253.	a. Run DMC
254.	c. *Can I Borrow A Dollar?*
255.	c. *From Where???*
256.	a. 1994
257.	b. "Five Minutes to Funk"
258.	a. Young MC
259.	b. The Genius/Gza
260.	b. *3 Feet High and Rising*
261.	c. Joe Ski Love
262.	b. Main Source
263.	c. Common Sense
264.	b. "The South Bronx"
265.	c. Nas
266.	c. *A Wolf in Sheep's Clothing*
267.	a. Enjoy Records
268.	b. *The Red Oktoba*
269.	c. The Neptunes

RHYMES

Hip hop lyrics are spoken in a special way
The most creative use of verbal language today
It's modern day poetry spoken in time
They're clever, witty and of course they rhyme
They tell stories that we all can relate
From getting arrested to finding a date
This chapter is about rhymes artists use
Which artist or what song will you choose?

270. Who said the following? "My mind's got a mind of it's own, sometimes I can't find it at home, it hides in the stove."

a. Redman

b. Ol' Dirty Bastard

c. Eminem

271. Who sang the following? "It seems, I'm like Keenan, pickin up on the Vibe that he ain't too happy, I could just see it in his eyes. I don't know if it's the chicks or how we dividin the loot. Time to pay his ass a visit 'fore he decide to get cute."

    a. Freddy Foxx

    b. Fat Joe

    c. Jay-Z

272. Who said this? "Relax and take notes, while I take tokes of the marijuana smoke. Throw you in a choke - gun smoke, gun smoke."

    a. Cypress Hill

    b. Notorious B.I.G.

    c. Big Pun

273. What artist said this lyric? "Once you hear the beat kick, with grooves so funky, they come with a speed stick."

    a. Cam'ron

    b. Dr. Dre

    c. Pete Rock

274.   Which rap group performed the song that
        featured the following line? "How do you
        know where I'm at when you haven't been
        where I've been, understand where I'm
        coming from?"

    a.   Public Enemy

    b.   NWA

    c.   Cypress Hill

275.   Who said this? "Follow procedures the crowd
        couldn't wait to see this. Nobody been this
        long awaited since Jesus. Who wouldn't
        believe this I heard the word on the street is.
        I'm still one of the deepest on the mic since
        Adidas."

    a.   Nas

    b.   Rakim

    c.   Big Daddy Kane

276.   Name this song: "Now this is the part where
        the rap breaks down. It's real intense, no one
        makes a sound. Everything looks like it's 8
        Mile now."

    a.   "Just Lose It"

    b.   "Like Toy Soldiers"

    c.   "Without Me"

277. Who sang this? "I know you gon' let me shine and get mine. I know you gon' let me in wit this nine."

    a. The Game

    b. Young Buck

    c. Kanye West

278. Name this song: "When we be up in the club, we be posting the back, when we be in the club, girls always come to the back."

    a. "In the Club"

    b. "Party and Bullsh*t"

    c. "Headsprung"

279. Who said this? "But then again I got a story. That's harder than the hardcore. Cost of the holocaust. I'm talkin' 'bout the one still goin' on."

    a. Public Enemy

    b. Paris

    c. Ice Cube

280. Who said these lines? "Fresh dress, like a million bucks, put on the Bally shoes and the fly green socks. Stepped out the house stopped short, oh no."

    a. Snoop Doggy Dogg

    b. Ludacris

    c. Slick Rick

281. Name this song: "Uh! I'm a nice dude, with some nice dreams, see these ice cubes, see these ice creams."

    a. "Beautiful"

    b. "Ghost Showers"

    c. "Drop It Like It's Hot"

282. What is the name of this song by 50 cent? "Let's party! Everybody stand up, everybody put your hands up. Let's party! Everybody bounce with me, some champagne and burn a little greenery."

    a. "Candy Shop"

    b. "In The Club"

    c. "Disco Inferno"

283.   What is the name of this Chingy single?
        "Peeps call me up, said it's a hotel party. Just
        bring the liquor, there's already eight
        shawties. I'm on my way, let me stop by the
        store. Got a 12 pack of Corona, plus an ounce
        of dro, ya know."

        a.   "Right Thurr"

        b.   "Balla Baby"

        c.   "Holidae Inn"

284.   Who stated this? "It's only right that I was
        born to use mics and the stuff that I write, is
        even tougher than dice."

        a.   Nas

        b.   Jay-Z

        c.   Snoop Doggy Dogg

285.   What is this song by Fabolous called? "I
        wanna be more than a friend to you now.
        When they ask, I mention my babygirl in the
        interviews now. And I don't bring the
        problems from the 980's and the 2 thou.
        There's no reason to have a friend or two
        now."

        a.   "Into You"

        b.   "Can't Let You Go"

        c.   "Baby"

286. What's the name of this single by Ja Rule? "Wanna keep you flawed with no dough, pimpin ain't easy. Trust me I know, when gangstas and ho's, Go go go go go go together"

    a. "Wonderful"

    b. "Thug Lovin"

    c. "Mesmerize"

287. This is the name of the song sung by Jay-Z. "Look for me! Young B, cruisin' down the Westside highway. Doing what we like to do our way. Eyes behind shades, this necklace the reason all of my dates been blind dates."

    a. "03' Bonnie & Clyde"

    b. "Change Clothes"

    c. "I Just Wanna Love You"

288. What is the name of this single by Ludacris? "It's the knick knack paddywhack, still ride in Cadilacs. Family off the street! Made my homies put the baggies back. Still stacking plaques! Still action packed! And dough! I keep it flipping like acrobats!"

    a. "Roll Out"

    b. "Stand Up"

    c. "Get Back"

289. **Which one of the following Nelly songs has these lyrics? "East coast, I know you're shakin' right Down south, I know you're bouncin' right West coast, I know you're walkin' right Midwest, I see you swingin' right."**

   a. "Dilemma"

   b. "My Place"

   c. "Over and Over"

290. **What is the song by T.I.? "TIP comin live from the VIP Heard the night life lost life when I leave Both and Feds and the State wanna see my need. The whole city got bizzerk he got treat."**

   a. "24's"

   b. "Bring 'Em Out"

   c. "You Don't Know Me"

291. **Who said this? "I know he hear me when my feet get weary."**

   a. DMX

   b. Kanye West

   c. KRS-One

292. Who said the following? "I feel like Bill Cosby pouring in the pudding."

    a. Jay-Z

    b. Nore

    c. Cam'ron

293. Who said the following? "I came back with some sicker stones that got these broke niggaz lookin' at me like they choking on a chicken bone."

    a. T.I.

    b. Fabolous

    c. Ludacris

294. What artist wrote this lyric? "We only humans, girl we make mistakes, to make it up I do whatever it takes. I love you like a fat kid love cake. You know my style I say anything to make you smile."

    a. Ludacris

    b. 50 cent

    c. Lloyd Banks

295. Who sang this? "Girl recognize game, before game recognize you. You're dealin wit a player, true. Now whatchu wanna do?"

   a. Chingy

   b. Jay-Z

   c. LL Cool J

296. Who said the following? "I thank the Lord everyday that I'm blessed with a gift. I'm the best, so, unless you wanna rest with the stiff."

   a. Nas

   b. DMX

   c. Ja Rule

297. Who said this? "I hate to brag, but damn I'm good and if mics were a gun, I'd be Clint Eastwood."

   a. KRS-One

   b. Redman

   c. Big Daddy Kane

298. Who said the following? "Some of y'all niggas hot, sike I'm gassin. Clowns I spot em and I can't stop laughin."

   a. Canibus

   b. Eve

   c. Lil Wayne

299. Who sang this? "Aiyyo,this rappin's like Ziti, facin' me real TV. Crash at high speeds, strawberry, kiwi."

   a. Ghostface

   b. Raekwon

   c. Ol' Dirty Bastard

300. What artist wrote this lyric? "Physical rap means we live the lyrics. Long as niggaz fear us you could never entirely disappear us. We the realest you ever gon' see. In all honesty, ain't another brother that's hotter than me."

   a. DMX

   b. 2pac

   c. Fat Joe

301. Who sang this? "You know the whole repertoire, U.S. to the U-S-S-R. Sexier than a Lexus car. Match wits with the best of y'all the rest of y'all, is like vegetables in my presence, check it."

   a. Jay-Z

   b. Big Daddy Kane

   c. Nas

302. Who sang this? "And now all you hookas and ho's know how I feel. Well if it's good enough to get broke off a proper chunk, I'll take a small piece of some of that funky stuff."

    a. Too Short

    b. 50 cent

    c. Snoop Doggy Dogg

303. What artist wrote this lyric? "Jealousy, we gotta swallow it. Your heart and mind, baby, follow it. Smile, happiness you can model it."

    a. Ja Rule

    b. Common

    c. LL Cool J

304. Who said the following? "My name alone been known to break up happy homes. No disrespect, dog, but you ain't have no business even answering her phone."

    a. Trick Daddy

    b. Ludacris

    c. Cam'ron

305. Who sang this? "It's a shame, you chose the dope game. Now you slang cane on the streets with no name. It was plain that your aim was mo' cane. You got game now you run with no shame."

   a. MC Hammer

   b. Nas

   c. 2pac

306. What artist sang this? "MC's can only battle with rhymes that got punch lines. Let's battle to see who headlines. Instead of flow for flow, let's go show for show, toe for toe, you, you better act like you know."

   a. Jay-Z

   b. KRS-One

   c. LL Cool J

307. The lyrics, "Some say the blacker the berry, the sweeter the juice. I say the darker the flesh, then the deeper the roots" come from which rap song?

   a. "Juicy" by Notorious B.I.G

   b. "Black Girl Lost" by Nas

   c. "Keep Ya Head Up" by 2pac

Peep This! Hip Hop Trivia

308. Who wrote this lyric? "MCs fear me, they too near not to hear me. Clearly, I'm the triple beam dream, one thousand grams of uncut to the gut."

    a. Notorious B.I.G.

    b. Fat Joe

    c. Jay-Z

309. Who said this? "Brain cells are lit, ideas start to hit. Next the formation of words that fit. At the table I sit, making it legit. And when my pen hits the paper, ahh sh*t!"

    a. Nas

    b. Big Daddy Kane

    c. Ice-T

310. What song are theses lyrics from? "Listen for lessons I'm saying inside music that the critics are blasting me for. They'll never care for the brothers and sisters now across the country has us up for the war."

    a. "Self Destruction"

    b. "Bring The Noise"

    c. "Don't Believe The Hype"

90

311. Who said "They did the job money came with ease but one couldn't stop, it's like he had a disease. He robbed another and another and a sista and her brotha tried to rob a man who was a D.T. undercover."

    a. Ice-T

    b. Ice Cube

    c. Slick Rick

312. Who said, "Girlies wanna ride with a brother like me cuz they be hear me gettin funky frequently"?

    a. Redman

    b. LL Cool J

    c. Lord Finesse

313. Who said this? "You caught an attitude, you need food to eat up. I'm scheming like I'm dreaming on a couch wit my feet up. You scream I'm lazy, you must be crazy. Thought I was a donut, you tried to glaze me."

    a. Rakim

    b. LL Cool J

    c. DJ Jazzy Jeff and The Fresh Prince

314. Who said these lyrics? "You had enough. I know you're overstuffed. If I keep going, you'll be throwin' up."

    a. KRS-One

    b. Kool Moe Dee

    c. Jadakiss

315. Who said this? "I rip shop in hip-hop I get props my lip rocks. The rap stuff's more spooky than movies from Hitchcock."

    a. Redman

    b. Twista

    c. Ol' Dirty Bastard

316. Who said this? "Most critically acclaimed Pulitzer prize winner best storyteller thug narrator my style's greater model dater, big threat to a lot of you haters commentators bring aside try watchin my paper."

    a. Notorious B.I.G.

    b. Nas

    c. 2pac

317. Who said? "Just waking up in the morning gotta thank God. I don't know but today seems kinda odd. No barking from the dogs no smog. And momma cooked a breakfast with no hog."

    a. Snoop Doggy Dogg

    b. KRS-One

    c. Ice Cube

318. Who stated, "The souls escaping, through this hole that its gaping. This world is mine for the taking. Make me king, as we move toward a new world order"?

    a. KRS-One

    b. Eminem

    c. Guru

319. Who said, "I've got the power to spread out and devour. At the same time I'll eat you up with a rhyme. But I'll let you slide cuz you accidentally hopped on the wrong side. Now come on, that's suicide"?

    a. Big Daddy Kane

    b. The DOC

    c. MC Lyte

320. Who stated, "Yeah in saloons we drink Boone's and battle goons till high noon. Bust rap toons on flat spoons, take no shorts like poon poon's"?

a. Lauryn Hill

b. Busta Rhymes

c. Q-tip

321. Who said the following? "I'm not an MC who' talkin' all that junk. About who can beat who, soundin' like a punk. I just get down and I go for mine. Say "Check 1-2" and run down a line."

a. Run-DMC

b. EPMD

c. LL Cool J

322. What Eric B. and Rakim song is this rhyme from? "I take 7 MCs put em in a line. And add 7 more before I go for mine. And that's 21 MCs ate up at the same time."

a. "My Melody"

b. "Move The Crowd"

c. "I Ain't No Joke"

323. Who said the following? "Now you younguns grow up buggin', any new jock you're huggin' weak production let me tell you somethin'. Any MC can battle for glory. But to kick a dope rhyme to wake up your people's another story."

    a. KRS-One

    b. Rakim

    c. LL Cool J

324. Who said this? "You know the evil that men do, hell is where the men go. We snatched him by his hands and feet and threw him out the window."

    a. Rza

    b. GangStarr

    c. Kool G. Rap

325. Who sings this chorus? "No, I ain't got no girlfriend
No, I ain't buy no car. No, I ain't got no babies. A lot of ladies. Naw, they want money."

    a. Eazy E

    b. Kool Moe Dee

    c. Ice-T

326. **Which song does Snoop say theses rhymes? "May I kick a little somethin' for the G's and make a few billions as I breeze through. Two in the mornin' and the party's still jumpin' 'cause my mama ain't home."**

    a. "Ain't Nuthin' But A G Thang"

    b. "Gin & Juice"

    c. "Party With A D.P.G."

327. **Who said the following? "You grow in the ghetto, living second rate. And your eyes will sing a song of deep hate. The places you play and where you stay, looks like one great big alleyway."**

    a. Scarface

    b. Fearless Four

    c. Grandmaster Flash and The Furious Five

328. **Who said the following? "cause havin' cash is highly addictive especially when you're used to havin' money to live with. I thought step back look at my life as a whole. Ain't no love it seems the devil done stole my soul."**

    a. Black Moon

    b. Mobb Deep

    c. M.O.P.

329.   10. Who said this? "There's gonna be a lot of
        slow singin' and flower bringin' if my burglar
        alarm starts ringin'."

        a.   Ice Cube

        b.   DMX

        c.   Notorious B.I.G.

330.   From which GangStarr song does Guru says
        these rhymes? "Rap is an art you can't own
        no loops. It's how you hook em up and the
        rhyme style troop. So don't even think you
        could say someone bit off your weak beat
        come on you need to quit."

        a.   "Mass Appeal"

        b.   "Take It Personal"

        c.   "You Know My Steez"

331.   What Mobb Deep song are these rhymes from?
        "Your simple words just don't move me
        you're minor, we're major you all up in the
        game and don't deserve to be a player don't
        make me have to call your name out."

        a.   "Survival Of The Fittest"

        b.   "Shook Ones Pt. 2"

        c.   "Drop A Gem On Em"

332. Who said the following? "I want me a mill, to see just how it feel. No worries bout no bills negotiating deals."

    a. Juvenile

    b. Special Ed

    c. MC Eiht

270.	c. Eminem
271.	c. Jay-Z
272.	b. Notorious B.I.G.
273.	b. Dr. Dre
274.	c. Cypress Hill
275.	b. Rakim
276.	a. "Just Lose It"
277.	b. Young Buck
278.	a. "In the Club"
279.	a. Public Enemy
280.	c. Slick Rick
281.	c. "Drop It Like It's Hot"
282.	c. "Disco Inferno"
283.	c. "Holidae Inn"
284.	a. Nas
285.	a. "Into You"
286.	a. "Wonderful"
287.	a. "03' Bonnie & Clyde"
288.	c. "Get Back"
289.	a. "Dilemma"
290.	b. "Bring Em Out"
291.	b. Kanye West
292.	c. Cam'ron
293.	b. Fabulous
294.	b. 50 cent
295.	a. Chingy
296.	b. DMX
297.	c. Big Daddy Kane
298.	b. Eve
299.	a. Ghostface
300.	c. Fat Joe
301.	a. Jay-Z
302.	c. Snoop Doggy Dogg
303.	b. Common

304.	a. Trick Daddy
305.	c. 2pac
306.	b. KRS-One
307.	c. "Keep Ya Head Up" by 2pac
308.	a. Notorious B.I.G.
309.	b. Big Daddy Kane
310.	b. "Bring The Noise"
311.	c. Slick Rick
312.	b. LL Cool J
313.	a. Rakim
314.	b. Kool Moe Dee
315.	a. Redman
316.	b. Nas
317.	c. Ice Cube
318.	b. Eminem
319.	c. MC Lyte
320.	a. Lauryn Hill
321.	b. EPMD
322.	a. "My Melody"
323.	a. KRS-One
324.	c. Kool G Rap
325.	b. Kool Moe Dee
326.	b. "Gin & Juice"
327.	c. Grandmaster Flash and The Furious Five
328.	b. Mobb Deep
329.	c. Notorious B.I.G.
330.	b. "Take It Personal"
331.	b. "Shook Ones Pt. 2"
332.	a. Juvenile

LIFE

Hip hop culture has been around now for more than 30 years and its recording artists are selling millions of records. Today hip hop stars aren't just recording artists; they are TV and movie stars and successful entrepreneurs. They own record labels, clothing lines and other various businesses. Hip hop culture in one way or another has influenced the way we speak, dress, dance, and think. This chapter is on the lives of hip hop artists and the various elements of hip hop culture.

333.   What city is Common from?

    a.   Chicago

    b.   Cleveland

    c.   Detroit

334.   Who took over at Uptown Records after Andre Harrell left for Motown?

    a.   Puff Daddy

    b.   Heavy D

    c.   Teddy Riley

335. **What actor played Russell Simmons in *Krush Groove*?**

    a. Wesley Snipes

    b. Laurence Fishburne

    c. Blair Underwood

336. **What record label did Andre Harrell work at before Uptown Records?**

    a. Sugar Hill

    b. Enjoy Records

    c. Def Jam

337. **What city does Bones, Thugs and Harmony hail from?**

    a. Compton

    b. Chicago

    c. Cleveland

338. **What label was Eve signed to before becoming a Ruff Ryder?**

    a. Def Jam

    b. Uptown

    c. Aftermath

339.   Where is Monie Love originally from?

    a. London, England

    b. East Orange, NJ

    c. New York, NY

340.   What classic hip hop film featured Crazy Legs and his posse, along with notable hip hop stars such as Grandmaster Flash and Fab Five Freddy, Dondi and other graffiti artists, and other hip hop culture greats?

    a. *Beat Street*

    b. *Graffiti Wars*

    c. *Wild Style*

341.   What are the four original elements of hip hop?

    a. Mceeing, Beatboxing, Djaying, Breakdancing

    b. Mceeing, Graffiti, Djaying, Beatboxing

    c. Mceeing, Graffiti, Djaying, Breakdancing

342.   Which rapper made an appearance in the movie *Breakin*?

    a. MC Hammer

    b. Ice-T

    c. Dr. Dre

343. **Where is Domino from?**

   a. Compton

   b. Oakland

   c. Long Beach

344. **Where is Trick Daddy from?**

   a. Atlanta

   b. Miami

   c. Houston

345. **Who was the rapper who was featured on the movie *Wildcats*?**

   a. LL Cool J

   b. Ice-T

   c. Will Smith

346. **Ice Cube and what artist starred in the movie *Trespass*?**

   a. Mack 10

   b. Ice-T

   c. Tone Loc

347. **Who directed the film *Wild Style*?**

   a. Fab Five Freddy

   b. Charlie Ahearn

   c. Hype Williams

348. **Who produced the film *Beat Street*? Who directed it?**

   a. Quincy Jones/Fab Five Freddy

   b. Harry Belafonte/Stan Lathan

   c. Sidney Poitier/Henry Chalfant

349. **Who was the first group to make a national TV appearance? On what show?**

   a. Funky 4 +1 on *Saturday Night Live* in 1981

   b. Grandmaster Flash & The Furious Five on *Soul Train*

   c. Sugarhill Gang on *The Tonight Show*

350. **What was the first major network news program to document hip hop?**

   a. *60 minutes*

   b. *20/20*

   c. *Dateline*

351. **Who is known for the invention of "scratching"?**

   a.   Grandmaster Flash

   b.   Grand Wizard Theodore

   c.   AJ Scratch

352. **What video featured Fab 5 Freddy in the background as a graffiti artist?**

   a.   The Message

   b.   Rapture

   c.   Feel The Heartbeat

353. **From what group did the duo Double Trouble come from?**

   a.   Fearless Four

   b.   Cold Crush Brothers

   c.   Funky 4 +1

354. **What rappers battled on the single episode of the 1984 television show *Graffiti Rock*?**

   a.   Kool Moe Dee vs. Busy Bee

   b.   Run DMC vs. Kool Moe Dee and Special K

   c.   Melle Mel vs. Busy Bee

355. **Who was the founder of Sugar Hill Records?**

    a. Bobby Robinson

    b. Sylvia Robinson

    c. Joey Robinson

356. **What record label is Spoonie Gee's uncle associated with?**

    a. Sugar Hill

    b. Enjoy

    c. Mercury

357. **Where was Kool Herc born?**

    a. Bronx, New York

    b. Kingston, Jamaica

    c. Port Au Prince, Haiti

358. **Who came up with the mixing technique of cueing the record with headphones while the other was still playing?**

    a. Grand Wizard Theodore

    b. Kool Herc

    c. Grandmaster Flash

359. **What was Afrika Bambaataa's first release on?**

    a. "Zulu Nation Throwdown Part 1"

    b. "Planet Rock"

    c. "Jazzy Sensation"

360. **Which one of these MCs is NOT from Canada?**

    a. Saukrates

    b. Choclair

    c. Father MC

361. **What year did Crazy Legs join the Rock Steady Crew?**

    a. 1976

    b. 1979

    c. 1980

362. **Before Kurtis Blow was known as an MC he was a…**

    a. Breakdancer

    b. Graffiti Artist

    c. DJ

363. **What's the name of the Kid n' Play movie where they switched identities?**

a. *Head Of The Class*

b. *Class Is In Session*

c. *Class Act*

364. **What is the name of Nelly's energy drink?**

a. Derrty

b. Pimp Juice

c. Lightning Fuel

365. **What is the name of Russell Simmons' clothing line for women?**

a. Phat Farm

b. Women's Phat Farm

c. Baby Phat

366. **Which on of these movies did Cam'ron NOT appear in?**

a. *State Property 2*

b. *Honey*

c. *Paid In Full*

367. **As a kid, what team was MC Hammer a ballboy for?**

a. Los Angeles Dodgers

b. Oakland A's

c. San Francisco Giants

368. **The sitcom *The Fresh Prince of Bel Air* starring Will Smith was loosely based on whose life?**

a. Will Smith

b. Benny Medina

c. Quincy Jones

369. **What was the name of the sitcom that Queen Latifah starred in?**

a. *The Single Life*

b. *Living Single*

c. *Singles*

370. **Which one of these is NOT a clothing line started by the rapper Nelly?**

a. Vokál

b. Pimp Wear

c. Apple Bottoms

371.   **What is the name of the movie that starred Yo! MTV Raps' Ed Lover and Doctor Dre?**

    a.   *Who Got Next?*

    b.   *Who's Gonna Take The Weight?*

    c.   *Who's The Man?*

372.   **After Krush Groove, Run DMC starred in another movie. What is the name of it?**

    a.   *Tougher Than Leather*

    b.   *King of Rock*

    c.   *Raising Hell*

373.   **What is the name of the hip hop movie Mario Van Peebles starred in?**

    a.   *Beat Street*

    b.   *Rappin'*

    c.   *Breakin'*

374.   **What is the name of the sitcom that starred LL Cool J?**

    a.   *In the House*

    b.   *Sparks*

    c.   *Where We Live*

375. What is the name of the movie that Nas was in with Steven Seagal?

    a. *Belly of the Beast*

    b. *Ticker*

    c. *The Glimmer Man*

376. Which one of these movies about hip hop dancing featured members of the singing group B2K?

    a. *Save The Last Dance*

    b. *Honey*

    c. *You Got Served*

377. Which of these legendary hip hop icons was NOT in the movie Beat Street?

    a. DJ Kool Herc

    b. Grandmaster Flash

    c. Afrika Bambaataa

378. Which of these Spike Lee movies did Queen Latifah have a role in?

    a. *Jungle Fever*

    b. *Do The Right Thing*

    c. *School Days*

379. Which one of these movies did rapper Afrika Baby Bambaataa of the Jungle Brothers have a part in?

a. *Juice*

b. *Strictly Business*

c. *Livin' Large*

380. Which of these movies did Busta Rhymes and Ice Cube have parts in?

a. *Boyz N' The Hood*

b. *Higher Learning*

c. *Friday*

381. In which of these movies did 2pac made his big screen debut?

a. *Poetic Justice*

b. *Juice*

c. *Above The Rim*

382. What rapper was originally supposed to have the lead role in *Menace 2 Society*?

a. Ice Cube

b. Ice-T

c. Tupac Shakur

383. Who played Nas' girlfriend in the movie *Belly*?

    a. Taral Hicks

    b. Chilli

    c. T-Boz

384. Which of these rappers does NOT have a clothing line?

    a. Eve

    b. Eminem

    c. Mase

385. Sean "Diddy" Combs and DMX were both raised in which New York neighborhood?

    a. Manhattan

    b. Yonkers

    c. Bronx

386. What movie did DJ Pooh get a co-writing credit with Ice Cube?

    a. *Barbershop*

    b. *Barbershop 2*

    c. *Friday*

387.   In the movie *Wild Style*, who played the role
        of the graffiti writer Zoro?

    a.   Lee Quinones

    b.   Fab Five Freddy

    c.   Jean Michel Basquiat

388.   Which of these dancers was NOT in the
        movie *Breakin*?

    a.   Bugaloo Shrimp

    b.   Crazy Legs

    c.   Shabba Doo

389.   Who were the first rap artists to win a
        Grammy?

    a.   Run DMC

    b.   Beastie Boys

    c.   DJ Jazzy Jeff and the Fresh Prince

390.   Who was known as the "King of Records"?

    a.   Kool Herc

    b.   Afrika Bambaataa

    c.   Grandmaster Flash

391. **What does the Wu-Tang Clan mean when they say "Shaolin"?**

    a. Staten Island

    b. Newark

    c. Manhattan

392. **What is the name of Wu-Tang's Clothing line?**

    a. Wu Fashions

    b. Wu Gear

    c. Wu Wear

393. **Before Grandmaster Caz was an MC, he was know as a...**

    a. DJ

    b. Breakdancer

    c. Graffiti Artist

394. **At what club did this famous battle take place: Cold Crush vs. Fantastic Five?**

    a. The Roxy

    b. The Disco Fever

    c. Harlem World

395. **Who was the first rapper to be signed to a major label?**

   a. Kurtis Blow

   b. Afrika Bambaataa

   c. Jimmy Spicer

396. **Scarface helped launch the career of which of these current southern heavyweights?**

   a. Juvenile

   b. Nelly

   c. Ludacris

397. **Which rapper had "Thuglife" across his stomach?**

   a. 2pac

   b. Eazy E

   c. Notorious B.I.G.

398. **Name the first hip hop artist to collaborate with James Brown?**

   a. Afrika Bambaataa

   b. Spoonie Gee

   c. Kurtis Blow

399. Who went on to success after winning a record deal in the Tin Pan Apple rap contest?

    a. Run-DMC

    b. The Disco 3

    c. LL Cool J

400. Who was the first female rapper to have a gold album?

    a. Queen Latifah

    b. Roxanne Shante

    c. Salt-n-Pepa

401. Which female rapper was the first to have a platinum selling album?

    a. Queen Latifah

    b. Yo Yo

    c. Da Brat

402. Which two people are considered to be the fathers of rap?

    a. Grandmaster Flash & Kool Herc

    b. Kool Herc and Afrika Bambaataa

    c. Afrika Bambaataa & Grandmaster Flash

403. **In the late 80's, what old school rapper had battles on wax with LL Cool J?**

    a. Kurtis Blow

    b. Melle Mel

    c. Kool Moe Dee

404. **What legendary hip hop producer is Heavy D's cousin?**

    a. DJ Premier

    b. Marly Marl

    c. Pete Rock

405. **Who discovered Das Efx?**

    a. Public Enemy

    b. Stetsasonic

    c. EPMD

333.   a. Chicago
334.   b. Heavy D
335.   c. Blair Underwood
336.   c. Def Jam
337.   c. Cleveland
338.   c. Aftermath
339.   a. London, England
340.   c. *Wild Style*
341.   c. Mceeing, Graffiti, Djaying, Breakdancing
342.   b. Ice-T
343.   c. Long Beach
344.   b. Miami
345.   a. LL Cool J
346.   b. Ice-T
347.   b. Charlie Ahearn
348.   b. Harry Belafonte/Stan Lathan
349.   a. Funky 4 +1 on *Saturday Night Live* in 1981
350.   b. *20/20*
351.   b. Grand Wizard Theodore
352.   b. Blondie's "Rapture"
353.   c. Funky 4 +1
354.   b. Run DMC vs Kool Moe Dee and Special K
355.   b. Sylvia Robinson
356.   b. Enjoy
357.   b. Kingston, Jamaica
358.   c. Grand Master Flash
359.   a. "Zulu Nation Throwdown Part I"
360.   c. Father MC
361.   a. 1979
362.   c. DJ
363.   c. *Class Act*
364.   b. Pimp Juice
365.   c. Baby Phat
366.   b. *Honey*

367.	b. Oakland A's
368.	b. Benny Medina
369.	b. *Living Single*
370.	b. Pimp Wear
371.	c. *Who's The Man?*
372.	a. *Tougher Than Leather*
373.	b. *Rappin'*
374.	a. *In The House*
375.	b. *Ticker*
376.	c. *You Got Served*
377.	b. Grand Master Flash
378.	a. *Jungle Fever*
379.	c. *Livin' Large*
380.	b. *Higher Learning*
381.	b. *Juice*
382.	c. Tupac Shakur
383.	c. T-Boz
384.	c. Mase
385.	b. Yonkers
386.	c. *Friday*
387.	a. Lee Quinones
388.	b. Crazy Legs
389.	c. DJ Jazzy Jeff and The Fresh Prince
390.	b. Africa Bambaataa
391.	a. Staten Island
392.	c. Wu Wear
393.	a. DJ
394.	c. Harlem World
395.	a. Kurtis Blow
396.	c. Ludacris
397.	a. 2pac
398.	a. Afrika Bambaataa
399.	b. The Disco 3 (a.k.a. The Fat Boys)
400.	a. Queen Latifah
401.	c. Da Brat
402.	b. Kool Herc and Afrika Bambaataa
403.	c. Kool Moe Dee

404.   c. Pete Rock
405.   c. EPMD

www.ingramcontent.com/pod-product-compliance
Lightning Source LLC
Chambersburg PA
CBHW030021290326
41934CB00005B/427